ARE WE REALLY CIVILIZED?

DILIP RAMANA

"Are We Really Civilized?"

Dilip Ramana

தனி ஒரு மனிதனுக்கு உணவில்லை எனில், ஜகெத்தினை அழித்திடுவோம் - மகாகவி பாரதி

"Irrespective of fluctuating global economic conditions, billionaires' net worth increase is a staggering $5.2 billion per day. At the same time 24,000 people die every single day from hunger. Shame on us." - The United Nations World Food Programme (WFP) Report

Chapter 1: Introduction to Civilization

Human history is a tapestry woven with threads of innovation, conflict, cooperation, and transformation. At the heart of this tapestry lies the concept of civilization, a complex and multifaceted idea that has shaped the course of human existence for several millennia. This chapter aims to explore the defining characteristics of civilization, trace its historical evolution, and introduce a crucial paradox: the irony of progress often juxtaposed with moral stagnation.

What Defines Civilization?

The term "civilization" evokes images of grand cities, intricate social hierarchies, and remarkable technological achievements. However, pinning down a precise definition remains a challenge, as the concept is fluid and subject to interpretation. Traditionally, several key characteristics have been used to identify a civilization:

- **Organized Government:** The establishment of formal political structures, including laws, institutions, and leadership roles, is a hallmark of civilization. Governments provide order, regulate social interactions, and manage resources. From early city-states to complex empires, organized governance has been essential for large-scale social organization.
- **Complex Social Structures:** Civilizations are characterized by social stratification, with distinct social classes and specialized roles. This includes rulers, priests, warriors, artisans, farmers, and labourers. This division of labour allows for greater efficiency and specialization but can also lead to social inequalities.
- **Advanced Technology:** Technological innovation is a driving force behind the development of civilizations. From the invention of agriculture and the wheel to the development of metallurgy and writing systems, technological advancements have transformed human societies and their relationship with the environment.
- **Development of Writing:** The invention of writing systems marked a pivotal moment in human history. It enabled the preservation of

knowledge, the transmission of information across generations, and the development of complex administrative and legal systems. Writing also facilitated the creation of literature, philosophy, and scientific thought.

- **Urban Centres:** Cities serve as hubs of economic, political, and cultural activity in civilized societies. They are centres of trade, manufacturing, and innovation, attracting populations from surrounding rural areas. The concentration of people in urban centres fosters social interaction, cultural exchange, and the development of specialized skills.
- **Specialized Labour:** The division of labour within a civilization leads to the emergence of specialized professions and crafts. Artisans, merchants, scribes, and other specialists contribute to the economic and cultural vibrancy of the society. This specialization allows for greater expertise and efficiency in various fields.
- **Shared Culture, Religion, and Art:** Civilizations are bound together by shared cultural values, beliefs, and artistic expressions. Religion often plays a central role in shaping social norms and providing a sense of collective identity. Art, architecture, literature, and music reflect the cultural values and aesthetic sensibilities of a civilization.

It is important to acknowledge that this list is not exhaustive, and the relative importance of each characteristic can vary between different civilizations. Furthermore, the concept of "civilization" has sometimes been used in a problematic way, to justify colonialism and the subjugation of other cultures deemed "uncivilized." A more nuanced understanding recognizes the diversity of human societies and avoids making value judgments based on a narrow definition of civilization.

The Historical Evolution of Civilizations

The emergence of the first civilizations marked a profound shift in human history. The transition from nomadic hunter-gatherer lifestyles to settled agricultural communities laid the foundation for the development of complex societies. The "Neolithic Revolution," beginning around 10,000 BCE, saw the domestication of plants and animals, enabling humans to produce their own food and establish permanent settlements.

The earliest civilizations arose in fertile river valleys: Mesopotamia (between the Tigris and Euphrates rivers), Egypt (along the Nile River), the Indus Valley (in present-day India and Pakistan), and China (along the Yellow River). These civilizations shared several common features:

- **Agricultural Surplus:** The development of agriculture led to surplus food production, which supported larger populations and allowed for specialization of labour.
- **Urbanization:** The growth of settled communities led to the development of cities, which became centres of trade, administration, and culture.
- **Social Hierarchy:** Social stratification emerged, with distinct social classes based on wealth, status, and occupation.
- **Political Organization:** Formal governments developed to manage resources, maintain order, and organize large-scale projects like irrigation systems and public works.

These early civilizations made significant contributions to human progress. The Sumerians in Mesopotamia developed cuneiform writing, the Egyptians built monumental pyramids and developed sophisticated mathematics and astronomy, the Indus Valley civilization created well-planned cities with advanced sanitation systems, and the Chinese developed sophisticated bronze technology and a complex writing system.

The rise and fall of civilizations throughout history demonstrate a cyclical pattern. Civilizations grow and prosper, reaching periods of great cultural and technological achievement, but they can also decline due to factors such as environmental degradation, internal conflict, external invasions, and economic instability. The lessons learned from the successes and failures of past civilizations offer valuable insights into the challenges and opportunities facing humanity today.

The Irony of Progress and Moral Stagnation

While the historical narrative of civilization is often presented as a story of continuous progress, a closer examination reveals a troubling paradox: the irony of technological and societal advancement occurring alongside persistent moral and ethical challenges. While humans have made remarkable strides in science, technology, and material well-being, issues like poverty, inequality, war, and environmental destruction continue to plague the world.

This book will explore this central paradox in detail. It will examine how, despite our advancements, we still struggle with fundamental questions of human dignity, justice, and compassion. It will question whether our technological prowess has truly translated into a more humane and equitable world. It will argue that a true civilization must be defined not only by its material achievements but also by its commitment to ethical principles and the well-being of all its members. The following chapters will delve into specific examples of this moral stagnation, exploring issues such as indifference to suffering, global hunger, poverty amidst wealth, and the consequences of a callous society. This exploration will serve as a call for a re-evaluation of what it truly means to be civilized and a plea for a future where humanity aligns its technological capabilities with a deep commitment to compassion and social justice.

Chapter 2: The Facade of Modernity

Modernity, with its dazzling array of technological marvels and seemingly boundless progress, presents a compelling narrative of human advancement. We live in an age where information travels at the speed of light, diseases once considered incurable are now treatable, and the boundaries of human knowledge are constantly expanding. Yet, beneath this gleaming veneer of progress lies a disquieting truth: a significant discrepancy between technological and societal advancement on one hand, and the cultivation of genuine humane values on the other. This chapter will delve into the facade of modernity, examining the remarkable progress we have made while simultaneously exposing the underlying brutality and ethical shortcomings that persist.

Examination of Modern Technological and Societal Advancements

The past few centuries have witnessed an unprecedented acceleration of technological and societal change. The Industrial Revolution, with its mechanization of production and advancements in transportation, ushered in an era of rapid industrial growth and urbanization. The 20th and 21st centuries have seen even more dramatic transformations, driven by breakthroughs in fields such as:

- **Medicine and Healthcare:** Advances in medical science have led to the eradication of some infectious diseases, the development of life-saving treatments, and significant increases in life expectancy. From vaccines and antibiotics to organ transplantation and genetic engineering, modern medicine has transformed human health and well-being.
- **Communication and Information Technology:** The invention of the telephone, the internet, and mobile devices has revolutionized communication, connecting people across the globe in ways unimaginable just a few decades ago. The internet has democratized access to information, fostering global collaboration and knowledge sharing.

- **Transportation and Infrastructure:** Modern transportation systems, including automobiles, airplanes, and high-speed trains, have shrunk the world, facilitating trade, travel, and cultural exchange. Advanced infrastructure, such as roads, bridges, and power grids, supports modern economies and improves living standards.
- **Science and Exploration:** Scientific research has expanded our understanding of the universe, from the smallest subatomic particles to the vast expanse of space. Space exploration has allowed us to venture beyond our planet, pushing the boundaries of human ingenuity and scientific discovery.

These advancements have undeniably improved many aspects of human life. We enjoy greater access to education, healthcare, and information than ever before. We can travel to distant lands, communicate with people across the globe, and access a wealth of knowledge at our fingertips. Modern technology has also created new opportunities for economic development, cultural exchange, and personal expression.

Discrepancy Between Progress and Humane Values

However, this narrative of unbridled progress masks a troubling reality. While we have achieved remarkable technological feats, the development of humane values has not kept pace. We continue to grapple with persistent social problems, including:

- **Poverty and Inequality:** Despite global economic growth, billions of people still live in poverty, lacking access to basic necessities like food, clean water, and healthcare. The gap between the rich and the poor continues to widen, creating social unrest and instability.
- **War and Conflict:** Despite the horrors of past wars, armed conflicts continue to erupt around the world, causing immense human suffering and displacement. The proliferation of weapons of mass destruction poses an existential threat to humanity.
- **Social Injustice and Discrimination:** Discrimination based on race, ethnicity, gender, religion, and other factors persists in many societies. Systemic inequalities continue to limit opportunities for marginalized communities.

- **Environmental Degradation:** The relentless pursuit of economic growth has led to widespread environmental damage, including climate change, deforestation, and pollution. The long-term consequences of this degradation threaten the health of the planet and the well-being of future generations.

This discrepancy between technological progress and the application of humane values raises fundamental questions about the nature of modernity. Has our focus on material advancement come at the expense of moral and ethical development? Have we become so enamoured with technological innovation that we have neglected the cultivation of compassion, empathy, and social justice?

How Societal Developments Mask Underlying Brutality

One of the most insidious aspects of the facade of modernity is the way in which societal developments often mask underlying brutality. Modern society has become adept at concealing and sanitizing the harsh realities faced by many. This masking occurs through several mechanisms:

- **Consumerism and Distraction:** The constant bombardment of advertising and the emphasis on consumerism create a culture of distraction, diverting attention from pressing social and environmental issues. Entertainment and media often serve as a form of escapism, allowing people to avoid confronting difficult realities.
- **Euphemisms and Sanitized Language:** Language is often used to sanitize and normalize acts of violence and injustice. For example, the term "collateral damage" is used to minimize the impact of civilian casualties in war. Economic policies that lead to poverty and inequality are often presented in abstract terms, obscuring their real-world consequences.
- **Spatial and Social Segregation:** The physical and social separation of different social classes and communities can create a sense of detachment and indifference to the suffering of others. The wealthy can often live in insulated environments, shielded from the realities of poverty and inequality.
- **Bureaucracy and Institutionalization:** The complex systems and institutions of modern society can create a sense of distance and

anonymity, making it easier to ignore the human cost of policies and decisions. The institutionalization of suffering, such as in prisons and detention centres, can further dehumanize individuals and make their plight invisible to the wider public.

By examining these mechanisms, we can begin to understand how the facade of modernity is maintained. We can see how the focus on technological progress and material comfort can obscure the underlying brutality and ethical shortcomings that persist in our societies. This understanding is crucial if we are to move beyond the facade and create a truly humane and just world. The following chapters will explore specific examples of this underlying brutality, examining issues such as indifference to suffering, global hunger, and the consequences of a callous society.

Chapter 3: Indifference and Apathy

In the midst of unprecedented technological advancement and interconnectedness, a disturbing phenomenon persists: a pervasive sense of indifference and apathy towards the suffering of others. This chapter delves into the complex dynamics of human indifference, exploring the psychological and sociological factors that contribute to our desensitization to poverty, pain, and injustice. Understanding the roots of this apathy is crucial for fostering a more compassionate and responsive society.

Analysis of Human Indifference Towards Suffering

Indifference, in this context, refers to a lack of concern, interest, or sympathy towards the suffering of others. It is not merely a passive state of unawareness but rather an active disengagement from the plight of those in need. Several factors contribute to this phenomenon:

- **Psychological Distancing:** One of the primary mechanisms through which we maintain indifference is psychological distancing. This involves mentally separating ourselves from the suffering of others, viewing them as different, distant, or less human. This can be achieved through dehumanization, stereotyping, and creating "us vs. them" narratives.
- **Cognitive Dissonance:** When confronted with information that challenges our existing beliefs or worldview, we often experience cognitive dissonance, a state of psychological discomfort. To reduce this discomfort, we may selectively ignore or downplay information that contradicts our beliefs, leading to a form of wilful ignorance.
- **Emotional Numbness:** Constant exposure to images and stories of suffering through media can lead to emotional numbness or compassion fatigue. This desensitization can make it difficult to empathize with the pain of others, even when confronted with direct evidence of their suffering.
- **Diffusion of Responsibility:** In situations where there are multiple potential helpers, the responsibility to act is often diffused among the group. This phenomenon, known as the bystander effect, can lead to

inaction, as individuals assume that someone else will take
responsibility.

- **Just-World Hypothesis:** The belief in a just world, where people get
what they deserve, can lead to blaming victims for their own
misfortunes. This allows us to maintain a sense of order and control in
the world but can also contribute to indifference towards those who
are suffering.

The Psychology Behind Desensitization to Poverty and Pain

Desensitization, the diminished emotional responsiveness to a stimulus after
repeated exposure to it, plays a significant role in our indifference to poverty
and pain. The constant barrage of images and stories of suffering in the media
can lead to a gradual erosion of empathy and compassion. Several factors
exacerbate this process:

- **Media Saturation:** The 24/7 news cycle and the proliferation of social
media expose us to a constant stream of suffering from around the
world. This overexposure can lead to a sense of numbness and a
diminished capacity to respond emotionally.
- **Framing and Representation:** The way in which suffering is portrayed
in the media can also contribute to desensitization. Sensationalized or
stereotypical portrayals can dehumanize victims and make it harder to
empathize with their experiences.
- **Psychological Defence Mechanisms:** We often employ psychological
defence mechanisms, such as denial, repression, and rationalization,
to protect ourselves from the emotional distress caused by witnessing
suffering. These mechanisms can lead to a form of selective attention,
where we filter out information that is emotionally overwhelming.
- **Normalization of Suffering:** In some contexts, poverty, violence, and
other forms of suffering become normalized, particularly within
marginalized communities. This normalization can lead to a sense of
resignation and a diminished expectation for change.

Case Studies Showcasing Societal Apathy

Numerous real-world examples illustrate the pervasive nature of societal
apathy:

- **Homelessness:** The widespread presence of homelessness in many cities is a stark example of societal indifference. Despite the visible suffering of those living on the streets, many people choose to ignore or avoid the issue, contributing to the perpetuation of the problem.
- **Refugee Crises:** The ongoing refugee crises around the world demonstrate a disturbing lack of global empathy. Despite the desperate plight of millions of people fleeing war, persecution, and natural disasters, many countries have been reluctant to offer refuge or provide adequate support.
- **Environmental Degradation:** The slow but steady destruction of the environment is another example of societal apathy. Despite the growing evidence of climate change and other environmental threats, many people continue to prioritize short-term economic gains over long-term sustainability.
- **Genocide and Mass Atrocities:** History is replete with examples of genocide and mass atrocities, where entire populations have been targeted for extermination. These horrific events often occur with a backdrop of widespread indifference and inaction from the international community.
- **The Bystander Effect in Emergencies:** Numerous studies have demonstrated the bystander effect in emergency situations. When a person is in need of help in a public place, the presence of other bystanders often decreases the likelihood that anyone will intervene.

These case studies highlight the devastating consequences of societal apathy. They demonstrate how indifference can allow suffering to persist and even escalate, leading to preventable tragedies. Overcoming this apathy requires a conscious effort to cultivate empathy, challenge our biases, and take action to address the root causes of suffering. It necessitates moving beyond the comfortable distance we create and acknowledging our shared humanity with those who are suffering.

Chapter 4: The Hunger Crisis

Amidst a world of unprecedented agricultural productivity and technological advancement in food production, the persistent reality of global hunger stands as a stark indictment of our collective failure to address fundamental issues of equity and access. This chapter delves into the multifaceted nature of the hunger crisis, exploring its devastating statistics, sharing the harrowing experiences of those on the frontlines of famine, and critiquing the systemic failures of global food distribution and the pervasive problem of food waste.

Global Hunger Statistics and Their Implications

The sheer scale of global hunger is staggering. According to the Food and Agriculture Organization of the United Nations (FAO) and other reputable organizations, hundreds of millions of people worldwide suffer from chronic undernourishment. These statistics represent more than just numbers; they represent human lives marked by daily struggles for survival, diminished potential, and profound suffering. The implications of these statistics are far-reaching:

- **Stunted Growth and Development:** Malnutrition, particularly in early childhood, has devastating long-term consequences for physical and cognitive development. Stunted growth, impaired brain function, and weakened immune systems are just some of the effects of chronic hunger.
- **Increased Susceptibility to Disease:** Malnourished individuals are far more vulnerable to infectious diseases. Their weakened immune systems are unable to effectively fight off infections, leading to increased rates of illness and mortality.
- **Economic and Social Costs:** Hunger and malnutrition have significant economic and social costs. They reduce productivity, hinder educational attainment, and perpetuate cycles of poverty. A hungry population is less able to contribute to economic growth and social development.
- **Humanitarian Crises:** In extreme cases, food shortages can lead to famine, a catastrophic situation characterized by widespread starvation and mass death. Famines often trigger humanitarian crises, requiring large-scale international intervention.

- **Intergenerational Impacts:** The effects of malnutrition can be passed down from one generation to the next. Malnourished mothers are more likely to give birth to underweight babies, perpetuating the cycle of hunger and poverty.

These statistics paint a grim picture of the global hunger crisis. They highlight the urgent need for concerted action to address the root causes of hunger and ensure that everyone has access to adequate nutritious food.

Stories from the Frontlines of Famine-Stricken Regions

Statistics, while essential for understanding the scope of the problem, can often obscure the human face of hunger. To truly grasp the devastating impact of food insecurity, it is crucial to hear the stories of those living on the frontlines of famine and chronic hunger:

- **The Mother Who Skips Meals:** Imagine a mother in a drought-stricken region, forced to choose between feeding her children and going hungry herself. She skips meals for days, her body weakening, just to ensure her children have something to eat. This is the daily reality for countless mothers around the world.
- **The Child with Swollen Belly:** Picture a child with a distended belly, a tell-tale sign of severe malnutrition. Their limbs are thin and weak, their energy depleted. They are vulnerable to infections and their future is uncertain. This image is a stark reminder of the devastating consequences of childhood hunger.
- **The Farmer Who Lost His Crops:** Envision a farmer who has lost his crops due to drought or flooding. His family's livelihood is destroyed, and they face the prospect of starvation. He is forced to make desperate choices, selling his meagre possessions or migrating in search of food.
- **The Refugee in a Crowded Camp:** Consider the plight of a refugee living in a crowded camp, dependent on food aid. The rations are meagre and often insufficient to meet their nutritional needs. They live in a constant state of uncertainty, unsure of where their next meal will come from.

These stories, while heart-breaking, are essential for humanizing the statistics and fostering empathy. They remind us that behind every number is a human being struggling for survival.

Critique of Global Food Distribution and Waste

The persistence of hunger in a world of abundant food production points to fundamental flaws in the global food system. The problem is not a lack of food but rather a lack of equitable access and efficient distribution. Several factors contribute to this problem:

- **Unequal Distribution:** Food is not distributed evenly around the world. Many developing countries, particularly in sub-Saharan Africa and South Asia, face chronic food shortages, while developed countries often have surpluses.
- **Food Waste:** A significant portion of food produced globally is wasted. In developed countries, much of this waste occurs at the consumer level, with food being discarded from households and restaurants. In developing countries, food losses often occur during production, storage, and transportation due to inadequate infrastructure and technology.
- **Market Forces and Speculation:** Global food prices are often subject to market forces and speculation, which can lead to price volatility and make food unaffordable for the poorest populations.
- **Conflict and Instability:** Armed conflicts and political instability disrupt food production and distribution, exacerbating hunger crises. Displacement of populations and destruction of infrastructure further compound the problem.
- **Climate Change:** The changing climate is increasingly impacting agricultural production, with more frequent droughts, floods, and extreme weather events. These climate-related shocks threaten food security, particularly in vulnerable regions.

Addressing the hunger crisis requires a multi-pronged approach that tackles these systemic issues. This includes:

- **Improving Food Distribution Networks:** Investing in infrastructure and logistics to improve the efficient and equitable distribution of food.
- **Reducing Food Waste:** Implementing measures to reduce food waste at all stages of the supply chain, from production to consumption.
- **Promoting Sustainable Agriculture:** Supporting sustainable agricultural practices that increase food production while protecting the environment.
- **Addressing Conflict and Instability:** Working to resolve conflicts and promote peace and stability, creating an environment conducive to food security.
- **Investing in Social Safety Nets:** Providing social safety nets, such as food assistance programs and cash transfers, to support vulnerable populations.

The hunger crisis is not an insurmountable problem. With concerted effort, political will, and a commitment to global justice, we can create a world where everyone has access to the nutritious food they need to thrive.

Chapter 5: Poverty Amidst Wealth

The coexistence of extreme wealth and abject poverty in the 21st century presents a stark and disturbing paradox. In a world characterized by unprecedented economic growth and technological advancement, millions continue to live in conditions of extreme deprivation, lacking access to basic necessities like food, clean water, shelter, and healthcare. This chapter examines the jarring contrast between affluence and destitution, explores the role of capitalism in perpetuating inequality, and amplifies the voices of those living in poverty, offering real-life testimonies that illuminate the human cost of this profound disparity.

The Stark Contrast Between Affluence and Destitution

The gap between the world's richest and poorest individuals has reached alarming proportions. While some enjoy unimaginable wealth, possessing multiple homes, private jets, and vast investment portfolios, others struggle to survive on less than a few dollars a day. This stark contrast manifests itself in numerous ways:

- **Access to Basic Necessities:** While the affluent can indulge in luxury goods and experiences, those living in poverty often lack access to basic necessities like clean water, nutritious food, adequate sanitation, and basic healthcare. Waterborne diseases, malnutrition, and preventable illnesses are tragically common in impoverished communities.
- **Housing and Shelter:** While the wealthy reside in spacious mansions and luxurious apartments, millions live in overcrowded slums, makeshift shelters, or on the streets. These inadequate living conditions expose them to health risks, extreme weather, and social instability.
- **Education and Opportunity:** While the affluent have access to the best schools and universities, children in impoverished communities often lack access to quality education. This lack of educational opportunity perpetuates cycles of poverty, limiting their future prospects and hindering social mobility.
- **Healthcare and Longevity:** While the wealthy can afford the best medical care, those living in poverty often lack access to basic

healthcare services. This disparity in healthcare access contributes to higher rates of infant mortality, maternal mortality, and lower life expectancy in impoverished communities.

- **Exposure to Environmental Hazards:** Impoverished communities are often disproportionately exposed to environmental hazards, such as pollution, contaminated water, and the effects of climate change. This environmental injustice further exacerbates their vulnerability and contributes to health problems.

This stark contrast is not merely a matter of differing lifestyles; it represents a fundamental inequality in access to resources and opportunities. It underscores the profound injustice of a system that allows some to accumulate vast wealth while others struggle to survive.

The Role of Capitalism in Perpetuating Inequality

The relationship between capitalism and inequality is complex and multifaceted. While capitalism has undoubtedly generated immense wealth and driven innovation, certain aspects of the system can also contribute to widening the gap between rich and poor:

- **Profit Maximization:** The inherent drive for profit maximization within capitalist systems can lead to exploitation of labour, environmental degradation, and the prioritization of short-term gains over long-term sustainability.
- **Concentration of Wealth:** Capitalism tends to concentrate wealth in the hands of a small elite. This concentration of wealth gives them disproportionate political and economic power, further exacerbating inequality.
- **Globalization and Neoliberal Policies:** Globalization, driven by neoliberal economic policies, has led to increased competition and deregulation, which can exacerbate inequalities between developed and developing countries and within societies.
- **Lack of Social Safety Nets:** In some capitalist systems, there is a lack of adequate social safety nets, such as unemployment benefits, healthcare, and affordable housing. This lack of support can leave vulnerable populations even more exposed to the risks of poverty.

- **Financialization and Speculation:** The increasing financialization of the global economy, with its emphasis on speculation and short-term profits, can contribute to economic instability and exacerbate inequalities.

It is important to note that not all forms of capitalism lead to the same degree of inequality. Countries with strong social welfare systems, robust labour protections, and progressive taxation policies tend to have lower levels of income inequality. However, the inherent tendencies of capitalism towards profit maximization and concentration of wealth must be addressed to mitigate its negative impacts on inequality.

Voices from the Impoverished: Real-Life Testimonies

Statistics and analyses, while important, can often fail to convey the human reality of poverty. To truly understand the impact of this disparity, it is crucial to listen to the voices of those who experience it first-hand:

- **The Single Mother Struggling to Make Ends Meet:** Imagine a single mother working multiple minimum-wage jobs, struggling to provide for her children. She worries constantly about paying rent, putting food on the table, and affording basic necessities. Her life is a constant struggle for survival.
- **The Homeless Person Living on the Streets:** Consider the experience of a homeless person living on the streets. They face daily challenges of finding food, shelter, and safety. They are often stigmatized and marginalized, further compounding their vulnerability.
- **The Rural Farmer Facing Drought and Debt:** Picture a rural farmer facing drought and mounting debt. Their crops have failed, and they are unable to repay their loans. They face the prospect of losing their land and being forced into further poverty.
- **The Child Working in a Sweatshop:** Imagine a child working long hours in a sweatshop, exposed to hazardous conditions for meagre pay. They are denied an education and robbed of their childhood. Their labour contributes to the profits of multinational corporations.

These testimonies, while diverse in their specifics, share a common thread: the experience of profound hardship, vulnerability, and a lack of control over one's own life. They underscore the urgent need to address the root causes of poverty and inequality. They remind us that behind the statistics are real people with real lives, hopes, and dreams.

Addressing the issue of poverty amidst wealth requires a fundamental shift in our thinking and a commitment to creating a more just and equitable world. This includes:

- **Addressing Systemic Inequalities:** Implementing policies that address the root causes of poverty, such as access to education, healthcare, and employment opportunities.
- **Strengthening Social Safety Nets:** Providing robust social safety nets to protect vulnerable populations from the worst effects of poverty.
- **Promoting Fair Trade and Economic Justice:** Advocating for fair trade practices and economic policies that promote greater equity and opportunity.
- **Challenging the Concentration of Wealth:** Implementing progressive taxation policies and other measures to address the excessive concentration of wealth.

By acknowledging the stark contrast between affluence and destitution, understanding the role of capitalism in perpetuating inequality, and amplifying the voices of those living in poverty, we can begin to pave the way for a more just and compassionate future.

Chapter 6: Suffering in Silence

While the previous chapters have explored the broader issues of poverty, hunger, and inequality, this chapter focuses on the often-unseen and unheard suffering experienced by marginalized communities. This suffering, frequently normalized or ignored by the dominant culture, takes many forms and has profound emotional, mental, and physical consequences for those who endure it. This chapter delves into the everyday struggles of these communities, examines how suffering becomes normalized in various cultural contexts, and explores the significant emotional and mental toll exacted on the victims.

The Everyday Struggles of Marginalized Communities

Marginalized communities are groups of people who are excluded from full participation in society due to various factors such as race, ethnicity, gender, sexual orientation, disability, socioeconomic status, or religion. The everyday struggles they face are often multifaceted and interconnected:

- **Discrimination and Prejudice:** Marginalized groups frequently experience discrimination and prejudice in various aspects of life, including employment, housing, education, and healthcare. This discrimination can manifest in overt acts of hostility or subtler forms of bias and exclusion.
- **Lack of Access to Basic Services:** Marginalized communities often lack access to essential services such as quality education, affordable healthcare, safe housing, and adequate infrastructure. This lack of access perpetuates cycles of poverty and limits opportunities for social mobility.
- **Social Exclusion and Isolation:** Marginalization can lead to social exclusion and isolation, as individuals are denied full participation in social, cultural, and political life. This isolation can have profound psychological consequences, leading to feelings of loneliness, alienation, and despair.
- **Economic Vulnerability:** Marginalized communities are often economically vulnerable, facing higher rates of unemployment, lower wages, and limited access to financial resources. This economic vulnerability can make them more susceptible to exploitation and hardship.

- **Exposure to Violence and Abuse:** Marginalized groups are often disproportionately exposed to violence and abuse, including domestic violence, hate crimes, and police brutality. This exposure can have devastating physical and psychological consequences.
- **Environmental Injustice:** Marginalized communities are often located in areas with higher levels of pollution, environmental hazards, and limited access to green spaces. This environmental injustice can contribute to health problems and further exacerbate their vulnerability.

These everyday struggles create a constant state of stress and hardship for individuals within marginalized communities. They are forced to navigate systemic barriers and overcome significant obstacles just to meet their basic needs and participate in society.

How Suffering is Normalized in Various Cultures

The normalization of suffering is a complex process that occurs within specific cultural contexts. Certain forms of suffering become accepted as part of the natural order or as an inevitable consequence of social structures. This normalization can make it difficult to challenge oppressive systems and advocate for change. Several factors contribute to this process:

- **Cultural Norms and Traditions:** Cultural norms and traditions can sometimes perpetuate harmful practices and inequalities. For example, certain cultural practices may condone gender-based violence or the exploitation of child labour.
- **Religious Beliefs and Interpretations:** Religious beliefs and interpretations such as fate and karma can sometimes be used to justify social hierarchies and inequalities. For example, certain interpretations of religious texts may be used to justify discrimination against women or LGBTQ+ individuals.
- **Historical Trauma and Intergenerational Transmission:** Historical trauma, such as slavery, colonization, or genocide, can have lasting effects on marginalized communities, leading to intergenerational transmission of trauma and a normalization of suffering.
- **Social and Political Power Dynamics:** The normalization of suffering is often linked to power dynamics within society. Those in positions of

power may use their influence to maintain the status quo and perpetuate inequalities, while those who are marginalized have limited power to challenge these systems.
- **Lack of Awareness and Understanding:** A lack of awareness and understanding of the experiences of marginalized communities can contribute to the normalization of their suffering. When the dominant culture is unaware of the challenges faced by these groups, it becomes easier to ignore or dismiss their plight.

This normalization of suffering can have a profound impact on individuals within marginalized communities. It can lead to internalized oppression, where individuals internalize negative stereotypes and accept their marginalized status. It can also lead to a sense of resignation and a diminished expectation for change.

Emotional and Mental Toll on the Victims

The constant experience of marginalization, discrimination, and hardship takes a significant emotional and mental toll on individuals. The psychological consequences of suffering in silence can be devastating:

- **Trauma and PTSD:** Exposure to violence, abuse, and discrimination can lead to trauma and post-traumatic stress disorder (PTSD). Symptoms of PTSD can include flashbacks, nightmares, anxiety, and hypervigilance.
- **Depression and Anxiety:** The chronic stress of living in marginalized conditions can contribute to depression and anxiety. Feelings of hopelessness, despair, and worthlessness are common.
- **Low Self-Esteem and Self-Worth:** Internalized oppression and negative stereotypes can lead to low self-esteem and a diminished sense of self-worth. Individuals may internalize negative messages about their identity and feel ashamed of their marginalized status.
- **Substance Abuse and Self-Harm:** Some individuals may turn to substance abuse or self-harm as coping mechanisms for dealing with the emotional pain of marginalization. These behaviours can have serious health consequences and further exacerbate their vulnerability.

- **Intergenerational Trauma:** The emotional and mental toll of marginalization can be passed down from one generation to the next. Children who grow up in marginalized communities may experience vicarious trauma and internalize the experiences of their parents and grandparents.

Addressing the suffering of marginalized communities requires a multi-faceted approach that addresses both the systemic causes of inequality and the individual experiences of trauma and hardship. This includes:

- **Challenging Systemic Discrimination:** Implementing policies and programs that address systemic discrimination and promote equality of opportunity.
- **Providing Mental Health Support:** Increasing access to culturally competent mental health services for marginalized communities.
- **Promoting Social Inclusion and Empowerment:** Creating opportunities for marginalized individuals to participate fully in social, cultural, and political life.
- **Raising Awareness and Understanding:** Educating the wider public about the experiences of marginalized communities and challenging stereotypes and prejudices.

By acknowledging the suffering that occurs in silence and taking action to address its root causes, we can create a more just and compassionate society where everyone has the opportunity to thrive.

Chapter 7: Disparity and Inequality

Disparity and inequality are not merely abstract concepts; they are deeply ingrained realities that shape the lives of individuals and communities across the globe. They represent a fundamental imbalance in the distribution of resources, opportunities, and power, leading to profound social, economic, and political consequences. This chapter provides a detailed analysis of economic and social disparities, examines the role of systemic structures in maintaining inequality, and explores the far-reaching impact of these disparities on social cohesion and global stability.

Analysis of Economic and Social Disparities

Economic disparity refers to the unequal distribution of wealth, income, and economic opportunities within a society or between different countries. Social disparity encompasses inequalities in access to education, healthcare, housing, justice, and other essential social goods. These two forms of disparity are often intertwined and mutually reinforcing. Several key indicators highlight the extent of these disparities:

- **Income Inequality:** Income inequality measures the gap between the incomes of the richest and poorest segments of society. The Gini coefficient is a commonly used measure of income inequality, with a score of 0 representing perfect equality and a score of 1 representing perfect inequality. Many countries exhibit significant levels of income inequality, with the top 1% of earners holding a disproportionate share of national income.
- **Wealth Inequality:** Wealth inequality refers to the unequal distribution of assets, such as property, stocks, and savings. Wealth is often even more concentrated than income, with a small percentage of the population owning a large share of the world's wealth.
- **Access to Education:** Disparities in access to quality education perpetuate social and economic inequalities. Children from disadvantaged backgrounds often lack access to good schools, educational resources, and opportunities for higher education.
- **Access to Healthcare:** Inequalities in access to healthcare contribute to disparities in health outcomes and life expectancy. People living in

poverty often lack access to affordable healthcare, leading to higher rates of preventable diseases and premature death.
- **Housing Inequality:** Disparities in access to safe and affordable housing contribute to social and economic inequalities. Many people struggle to find adequate housing, forcing them to live in overcrowded slums, makeshift shelters, or on the streets.
- **Justice and Legal Systems:** Inequalities in access to justice and legal representation can lead to unfair treatment and discrimination within the legal system. Marginalized communities are often disproportionately affected by crime and incarceration.

These indicators paint a clear picture of the pervasive nature of disparity and inequality. They demonstrate that these are not isolated problems but rather systemic issues that affect all aspects of society.

The Role of Systemic Structures in Maintaining Inequality

Inequality is not simply a result of individual choices or circumstances; it is deeply embedded within the structures and institutions of society. Systemic factors play a crucial role in maintaining and perpetuating inequality:

- **Historical Legacies:** Historical events, such as colonialism, slavery, and segregation, have created lasting inequalities that continue to shape contemporary society. These historical legacies have created systemic disadvantages for certain groups, perpetuating cycles of poverty and marginalization.
- **Economic Policies:** Economic policies, such as tax policies, trade agreements, and labour regulations, can have a significant impact on inequality. Policies that favour the wealthy or corporations can exacerbate income and wealth inequality.
- **Social Institutions:** Social institutions, such as education systems, healthcare systems, and legal systems, can also contribute to inequality. If these institutions are not accessible or equitable, they can perpetuate existing disparities.
- **Discriminatory Laws and Practices:** Discriminatory laws and practices, based on race, ethnicity, gender, sexual orientation, or other factors, can create systemic barriers to equality. These discriminatory

practices can limit opportunities for marginalized groups in employment, housing, education, and other areas of life.

- **Power Dynamics and Social Hierarchies:** Power dynamics and social hierarchies within society can reinforce inequality. Those in positions of power may use their influence to maintain the status quo and perpetuate existing disparities.

Understanding the role of these systemic structures is crucial for addressing inequality effectively. It requires moving beyond individualistic explanations and focusing on the broader social, economic, and political context.

Impact on Social Cohesion and Global Stability

Disparity and inequality have far-reaching consequences for social cohesion and global stability:

- **Social Unrest and Conflict:** High levels of inequality can lead to social unrest, protests, and even violent conflict. When a significant portion of the population feels marginalized and excluded, it can create social tensions and instability.
- **Erosion of Trust and Social Capital:** Inequality can erode trust and social capital within communities. When people feel that the system is unfair or that they are being treated unjustly, it can damage social cohesion and lead to a breakdown in social trust.
- **Political Instability and Corruption:** Inequality can contribute to political instability and corruption. When wealth and power are concentrated in the hands of a small elite, it can undermine democratic institutions and create opportunities for corruption.
- **Economic Instability and Crises:** Extreme levels of inequality can contribute to economic instability and financial crises. When a large portion of the population lacks purchasing power, it can lead to economic stagnation and vulnerability to economic shocks.
- **Global Instability and Migration:** Global inequalities can contribute to international tensions and migration flows. People living in impoverished or conflict-ridden countries may seek better opportunities in wealthier nations, leading to migration pressures and political tensions.

Addressing disparity and inequality is therefore not only a matter of social justice but also a matter of maintaining social cohesion and global stability. It requires a concerted effort to address the systemic causes of inequality and create a more just and equitable world. This includes:

- **Implementing Progressive Economic Policies:** Implementing tax policies, social welfare programs, and labour regulations that promote greater economic equality.
- **Strengthening Social Institutions:** Ensuring that social institutions, such as education and healthcare systems, are accessible and equitable for all.
- **Combating Discrimination and Promoting Inclusion:** Implementing laws and policies that prohibit discrimination and promote social inclusion for all groups.
- **Promoting Global Cooperation and Development:** Working to address global inequalities through international cooperation, development aid, and fair trade practices.

By recognizing the pervasive nature of disparity and inequality, understanding the role of systemic structures, and acknowledging the impact on social cohesion and global stability, we can begin to pave the way for a more just and equitable future. The following chapters will delve into the consequences of societal callousness, explore pathways towards compassion, and ultimately call for a redefinition of what it means to be civilized.

Chapter 8: Case Studies of Callousness

While previous chapters have analysed the systemic and societal factors contributing to suffering and inequality, this chapter focuses on specific instances of human callousness. By examining detailed case studies of cruelty and neglect from different parts of the world and historical periods, we aim to understand the human capacity for inflicting harm and the devastating consequences of indifference. These examples serve not to sensationalize violence but to illuminate the depths of human callousness and to underscore the urgent need for empathy and compassion.

Detailed Accounts of Human Cruelty and Neglect

The following case studies illustrate various forms of callousness, ranging from individual acts of cruelty to systemic forms of oppression and neglect:

- **The Rwandan Genocide (1994):** In a span of just 100 days, an estimated 800,000 people, primarily Tutsi, were systematically murdered in Rwanda. This genocide was fuelled by ethnic hatred, political opportunism, and widespread indifference from the international community. Neighbours turned against neighbours, and the world stood by as unimaginable atrocities were committed. The sheer brutality of the killings, often carried out with machetes, and the speed at which the genocide unfolded, shocked the world and exposed the depths of human cruelty. The international community's delayed response and failure to intervene effectively stand as a stark example of global callousness.
- **The Bengal Famine of 1943:** During World War II, a devastating famine struck Bengal, then part of British India, resulting in the deaths of an estimated 3 million people. While natural factors like crop failure contributed to the famine, human actions, particularly British wartime policies that prioritized resource allocation for the war effort, exacerbated the crisis. The callous disregard for the suffering of the Bengali population, evidenced by the inadequate relief efforts and the continued export of food from India, demonstrates how political and economic priorities can overshadow basic human needs.
- **The Exploitation of Child Labour in the Congo's Cobalt Mines:** The Democratic Republic of Congo is a major source of cobalt, a key

component in batteries for electronic devices and electric vehicles. However, the extraction of this valuable mineral is often carried out under horrific conditions, involving widespread exploitation of child labour. Children as young as seven years old work in dangerous mines, exposed to toxic dust and the risk of cave-ins. The global demand for electronic devices fuels this exploitation, highlighting the callous disregard for the well-being of these children in the pursuit of technological progress and profit.

- **The Syrian Civil War and the Refugee Crisis:** The ongoing Syrian civil war has resulted in a humanitarian catastrophe, with millions of people displaced and hundreds of thousands killed. The use of chemical weapons, the targeting of civilians, and the siege of cities have demonstrated a shocking disregard for human life. The resulting refugee crisis has placed immense strain on neighbouring countries and has been met with a mixed response from the international community, with some nations showing compassion while others have adopted restrictive policies, further exacerbating the suffering of refugees.

- **The Flint Water Crisis (2014-Present):** In Flint, Michigan, a change in the city's water source led to widespread lead contamination of the drinking water. This crisis exposed systemic failures in government oversight and a callous disregard for the health and well-being of the city's predominantly low-income and minority residents. The long-term health consequences of lead exposure, particularly for children, are devastating, and the slow response to the crisis demonstrated a lack of urgency and accountability.

Examples from Different Parts of the World

These case studies, while diverse in their specific contexts, demonstrate that callousness is not confined to any particular region, culture, or historical period. It is a universal human capacity that can manifest in various forms, from individual acts of violence to systemic forms of oppression and neglect. Examining examples from different parts of the world underscores the global nature of this problem and the need for a global response.

Reflection on the Human Capacity for Ruthless Behaviour

These case studies raise profound questions about the human capacity for ruthless behaviour. What factors contribute to individuals and groups acting with such cruelty and indifference? Several factors can contribute to this phenomenon:

- **Dehumanization:** Dehumanizing the "other" makes it easier to inflict harm. When individuals or groups are seen as less than human, it removes the moral constraints that would normally prevent violence and cruelty.
- **Ideology and Propaganda:** Ideologies and propaganda can be used to justify violence and dehumanization. These narratives can create a sense of moral righteousness, making it easier for individuals to commit atrocities in the name of a cause.
- **Power and Authority:** The abuse of power and authority can lead to acts of cruelty and neglect. When individuals or institutions have unchecked power, they can act with impunity, disregarding the well-being of those under their control.
- **Social Conformity and Group Pressure:** Social conformity and group pressure can play a significant role in perpetuating cruelty. Individuals may conform to the norms of their group, even if those norms involve violence or oppression.
- **Indifference and Apathy:** As discussed in previous chapters, indifference and apathy can create a permissive environment for cruelty. When people are indifferent to the suffering of others, it becomes easier for perpetrators to act without fear of consequences.

Understanding these factors is crucial for preventing future acts of callousness. It requires addressing the root causes of prejudice, discrimination, and inequality, as well as promoting empathy, compassion, and respect for human dignity. By confronting these dark aspects of human behaviour, we can work towards building a more just and humane world.

Chapter 9: The Cost of Ruthlessness

Ruthlessness, characterized by a lack of compassion or pity, and often accompanied by a willingness to exploit or harm others for personal gain, carries a heavy cost for individuals, societies, and the planet. This chapter explores the multifaceted consequences of a callous society, examining its long-term impact on global health, peace and security, and the environment. Understanding these costs is essential for motivating a shift towards a more compassionate and sustainable future.

The Consequences of a Callous Society

A society marked by ruthlessness suffers in numerous ways. The erosion of empathy and compassion weakens the social fabric, creating a climate of distrust, division, and conflict. The consequences manifest across various dimensions:

- **Erosion of Social Trust:** Ruthlessness undermines social trust, the foundation upon which healthy communities are built. When individuals and institutions prioritize self-interest over the well-being of others, it erodes trust in government, businesses, and even interpersonal relationships. This lack of trust can lead to social fragmentation, making it difficult to address collective challenges.
- **Increased Social Conflict:** A callous society is more prone to social conflict. When empathy and compassion are lacking, it becomes easier to dehumanize and demonize "the other," leading to increased prejudice, discrimination, and violence. This can manifest in various forms, from hate crimes and social unrest to armed conflict and war.
- **Decline in Mental and Physical Health:** Living in a ruthless society can have detrimental effects on mental and physical health. The constant stress of social conflict, economic insecurity, and lack of social support can lead to increased rates of anxiety, depression, and other mental health problems. Furthermore, a lack of access to healthcare and social services can exacerbate physical health problems, particularly for vulnerable populations.
- **Weakening of Democratic Institutions:** Ruthlessness can weaken democratic institutions. When political leaders and institutions prioritize self-interest and disregard the needs of the people, it

undermines public trust in government and erodes the foundations of democracy. This can lead to corruption, authoritarianism, and social instability.

- **Economic Inequality and Instability:** A callous approach to economic policy, prioritizing profit maximization over social well-being, can exacerbate economic inequality and lead to instability. This can manifest in widening income gaps, job losses, and economic crises.

Long-Term Impact on Global Health, Peace, and Security

The consequences of ruthlessness extend beyond individual societies, impacting global health, peace, and security:

- **Global Health Crises:** A lack of global cooperation and compassion can hinder efforts to address global health crises. The COVID-19 pandemic demonstrated how a lack of coordinated global response and equitable vaccine distribution can prolong a pandemic and exacerbate its impact on vulnerable populations. A callous approach to global health can lead to preventable suffering and death.
- **Increased Risk of Conflict and War:** Ruthlessness in international relations can increase the risk of conflict and war. When nations prioritize self-interest and disregard international law and human rights, it can lead to escalating tensions and armed conflict. The human cost of war, including loss of life, displacement, and destruction of infrastructure, is immense.
- **Threats to International Security:** Ruthlessness can contribute to various threats to international security, including terrorism, organized crime, and the proliferation of weapons of mass destruction. When individuals and groups operate without moral constraints, they are more likely to engage in violent and destabilizing activities.
- **Humanitarian Crises and Displacement:** A callous response to humanitarian crises can exacerbate suffering and lead to mass displacement. When nations are unwilling to provide adequate aid or offer refuge to those fleeing conflict or disaster, it creates immense human suffering and destabilizes entire regions.

Environmental Degradation Linked to Ruthless Exploitation

The ruthless pursuit of economic growth and profit, without regard for environmental consequences, has led to widespread environmental degradation:

- **Climate Change:** The burning of fossil fuels, deforestation, and other environmentally destructive practices have contributed to climate change, with devastating consequences for the planet. Rising sea levels, extreme weather events, and loss of biodiversity are just some of the impacts of climate change. A callous disregard for the environment threatens the well-being of current and future generations.
- **Resource Depletion:** The ruthless exploitation of natural resources, such as forests, minerals, and water, has led to depletion and environmental degradation. This unsustainable consumption of resources threatens the long-term health of ecosystems and the availability of resources for future generations.
- **Pollution and Environmental Degradation:** Industrial pollution, agricultural runoff, and improper waste disposal have led to widespread pollution of air, water, and soil. This pollution has detrimental effects on human health and the environment. A callous disregard for environmental protection exacerbates these problems.
- **Loss of Biodiversity:** The destruction of habitats and the overexploitation of species have led to a significant loss of biodiversity. This loss threatens the stability of ecosystems and the essential services they provide. A ruthless approach to economic development, prioritizing short-term gains over long-term sustainability, accelerates this loss.

The environmental consequences of ruthlessness are not merely abstract concerns; they have real and tangible impacts on human lives and livelihoods. Climate change, resource depletion, and pollution disproportionately affect vulnerable populations, exacerbating existing inequalities and creating new forms of hardship.

Addressing the cost of ruthlessness requires a fundamental shift in our values and priorities. We must move away from a culture of self-interest and exploitation towards a culture of compassion, empathy, and sustainability. This involves:

- **Promoting Global Cooperation and Solidarity:** Fostering international cooperation to address global challenges such as climate change, poverty, and conflict.
- **Strengthening International Institutions:** Supporting international institutions that promote peace, security, and human rights.
- **Investing in Sustainable Development:** Promoting sustainable economic development that protects the environment and ensures the well-being of future generations.
- **Cultivating Empathy and Compassion:** Promoting education and social programs that cultivate empathy, compassion, and respect for human dignity.

By recognizing the far-reaching consequences of ruthlessness and actively promoting compassion and sustainability, we can begin to mitigate its devastating costs and build a more just and harmonious world.

Chapter 10: The Path to Compassion

The preceding chapters have painted a stark picture of the consequences of callousness and the pervasive suffering that exists in our world. However, this is not a story of despair. Humanity possesses an immense capacity for compassion, and it is this capacity that offers a path towards a more just and humane future. This chapter explores potential solutions and interventions aimed at fostering greater compassion, emphasizing the importance of empathy and solidarity, and encouraging a shift towards a truly humane civilization.

Potential Solutions and Interventions

Cultivating compassion requires a multi-faceted approach that addresses individual attitudes, social structures, and global systems. Several potential solutions and interventions can contribute to this shift:

- **Education and Awareness:** Education plays a crucial role in fostering empathy and understanding. Educational programs that promote critical thinking, intercultural understanding, and human rights can help to challenge prejudices and cultivate compassion. Raising awareness about the suffering of others through storytelling, documentaries, and other forms of media can also help to break down indifference.
- **Promoting Empathy and Perspective-Taking:** Empathy, the ability to understand and share the feelings of others, is a cornerstone of compassion. Programs that promote empathy and perspective-taking, such as role-playing exercises, simulations, and community service projects, can help individuals to develop a deeper understanding of the experiences of others.
- **Cultivating Mindfulness and Emotional Intelligence:** Mindfulness practices, such as meditation and yoga, can help individuals to become more aware of their own emotions and the emotions of others. Developing emotional intelligence, the ability to understand and manage emotions effectively, can also contribute to greater compassion.
- **Strengthening Social Connections and Community Building:** Building strong social connections and fostering a sense of community can help

to reduce social isolation and promote empathy. Community-based programs that bring people from different backgrounds together can help to break down stereotypes and build bridges of understanding.

- **Promoting Ethical Leadership and Governance:** Ethical leadership and good governance are essential for creating a compassionate society. Leaders who prioritize the well-being of all citizens and uphold human rights can create a more just and equitable society. Transparent and accountable institutions can also help to prevent corruption and abuse of power.
- **Addressing Systemic Inequalities:** Addressing systemic inequalities, such as poverty, discrimination, and lack of access to education and healthcare, is crucial for creating a more compassionate society. Policies that promote economic justice, social inclusion, and equal opportunity can help to reduce suffering and create a more equitable world.
- **Promoting Global Cooperation and Solidarity:** Global challenges, such as climate change, poverty, and conflict, require global cooperation and solidarity. International agreements, development aid, and humanitarian assistance can help to address these challenges and promote a more just and sustainable world.

The Importance of Empathy and Solidarity

Empathy and solidarity are essential for building a compassionate society. Empathy allows us to connect with the suffering of others, while solidarity motivates us to take action to alleviate that suffering.

- **Empathy as a Catalyst for Action:** Empathy is not merely a passive feeling; it is a catalyst for action. When we empathize with the suffering of others, we are more likely to be motivated to help. Empathy can inspire acts of kindness, generosity, and social activism.
- **Solidarity as a Collective Force:** Solidarity, the feeling of unity and shared responsibility with others, is a powerful force for social change. When people come together in solidarity, they can achieve collective goals that would be impossible to achieve individually. Social movements, advocacy groups, and community organizations are examples of how solidarity can be used to promote social justice and alleviate suffering.

- **Breaking Down Barriers and Building Bridges:** Empathy and solidarity can help to break down barriers between different groups and build bridges of understanding. When we empathize with people from different backgrounds, we can overcome prejudices and stereotypes. Solidarity can create a sense of shared humanity, transcending differences in race, ethnicity, religion, and other factors.

Encouraging a Shift Towards a More Humane Civilization

Creating a more humane civilization requires a fundamental shift in our values, priorities, and behaviours. This shift involves:

- **Prioritizing Human Well-being over Material Gain:** Moving away from a culture that prioritizes material wealth and consumption towards a culture that values human well-being and social justice. This involves challenging the dominant narratives of consumerism and embracing a more sustainable and equitable way of life.
- **Upholding Human Rights and Dignity:** Respecting the inherent dignity and human rights of all individuals, regardless of their background or circumstances. This involves combating discrimination, promoting equality, and ensuring access to basic necessities for all.
- **Embracing Interconnectedness and Global Citizenship:** Recognizing our interconnectedness as global citizens and taking responsibility for the well-being of the planet and all its inhabitants. This involves promoting global cooperation, addressing climate change, and working towards a more sustainable future.
- **Cultivating a Culture of Compassion and Kindness:** Fostering a culture that values compassion, kindness, and empathy. This involves promoting positive social norms, encouraging acts of kindness, and celebrating the contributions of those who work to alleviate suffering.
- **Challenging Indifference and Apathy:** Actively challenging indifference and apathy towards the suffering of others. This involves raising awareness, promoting empathy, and encouraging action.

This shift towards a more humane civilization is not a utopian dream; it is a necessary and achievable goal. By cultivating compassion, embracing solidarity, and working together, we can create a world where everyone has the opportunity to thrive. The concluding chapter will summarize the key findings and insights of this exploration and offer a vision for a future where humanity aligns with compassion.

Chapter 11: Conclusion – Redefining Civilization

This exploration has traversed the complex landscape of human progress, examining the paradox of technological advancement juxtaposed with persistent moral and ethical challenges. We have delved into the stark realities of indifference, hunger, poverty, and the consequences of a callous society. However, this journey has not been one of despair but rather a call to action, a plea for a fundamental re-evaluation of what it means to be civilized. This concluding chapter summarizes the key findings and insights of this exploration, calling for a redefinition of civilization based on compassion, empathy, and social justice, and offering a vision for a future where humanity aligns with these core values.

Summarizing the Findings and Insights

Throughout this exploration, several key themes have emerged:

- **The Paradox of Progress:** While humanity has made remarkable strides in science, technology, and material well-being, these advancements have not been matched by a corresponding development in moral and ethical values. Issues such as poverty, inequality, conflict, and environmental degradation persist, highlighting the gap between technological progress and human compassion.
- **The Pervasiveness of Indifference:** Indifference and apathy towards the suffering of others are significant obstacles to creating a more humane world. Psychological distancing, desensitization, and systemic factors contribute to this indifference, allowing suffering to persist and even escalate.
- **The Devastating Impact of Inequality:** Economic and social disparities create profound inequalities in access to resources, opportunities, and power. These inequalities have far-reaching consequences for social cohesion, global stability, and the well-being of individuals and communities.
- **The Human Cost of Callousness:** Case studies of human cruelty and neglect have demonstrated the devastating consequences of a callous society. From genocide and famine to exploitation and environmental

destruction, ruthlessness carries a heavy cost for individuals, societies, and the planet.

- **The Power of Compassion:** Despite the challenges, humanity possesses an immense capacity for compassion. Cultivating empathy, promoting solidarity, and addressing systemic inequalities are essential steps towards creating a more just and humane world.

These insights underscore the urgent need for a fundamental shift in our understanding of civilization. We must move beyond a narrow focus on material achievements and embrace a broader vision that prioritizes human well-being, social justice, and environmental sustainability.

Calling for a Re-evaluation of What It Means to Be Civilized

The traditional definition of civilization, often focused on material progress, technological advancement, and the development of complex social structures, is insufficient. While these elements are undoubtedly important, they do not fully capture the essence of a truly civilized society. We must expand our definition to include core values such as:

- **Compassion and Empathy:** A truly civilized society prioritizes compassion and empathy, recognizing the inherent dignity and worth of all individuals. It actively seeks to alleviate suffering and promote the well-being of all its members.
- **Social Justice and Equality:** A civilized society strives for social justice and equality, ensuring that all individuals have equal access to resources, opportunities, and power. It actively combats discrimination and promotes inclusion.
- **Respect for Human Rights:** Upholding human rights is a fundamental principle of a civilized society. This includes protecting basic rights such as the right to life, liberty, and security, as well as promoting social, economic, and cultural rights.
- **Environmental Stewardship:** A civilized society recognizes its responsibility to protect the environment and ensure the sustainability of the planet for future generations. It promotes sustainable practices and actively combats environmental degradation.
- **Global Cooperation and Solidarity:** A civilized society embraces global cooperation and solidarity, recognizing the interconnectedness of

humanity and the need to address global challenges collectively. It promotes peace, diplomacy, and international cooperation.

This redefinition of civilization challenges us to move beyond a narrow focus on material progress and embrace a more holistic and humane vision. It calls for a fundamental shift in our values, priorities, and behaviours.

Vision for a Future Where Humanity Aligns with Compassion

The vision for a future where humanity aligns with compassion is not a utopian fantasy but a realistic and achievable goal. It is a future where:

- **Suffering is Minimized:** Through concerted efforts to address poverty, inequality, and conflict, suffering is significantly reduced. Global hunger is eradicated, and all individuals have access to basic necessities.
- **Human Rights Are Universal:** Human rights are universally respected and upheld. Discrimination and prejudice are actively combated, and all individuals are treated with dignity and respect.
- **The Environment is Protected:** The environment is protected and cherished. Sustainable practices are adopted globally, and the planet's resources are managed responsibly for future generations.
- **Peace and Cooperation Prevail:** Peace and cooperation prevail in international relations. Conflicts are resolved through diplomacy and dialogue, and global challenges are addressed collectively.
- **Empathy and Compassion Guide Actions:** Empathy and compassion guide individual and collective actions. People are motivated by a deep sense of shared humanity and a desire to alleviate suffering.

Achieving this vision requires a collective effort from individuals, communities, governments, and international organizations. It requires:

- **Individual Transformation:** Cultivating empathy, compassion, and ethical awareness in our daily lives. Challenging our own biases and prejudices and actively promoting kindness and understanding.
- **Social and Cultural Change:** Promoting social norms and cultural values that prioritize compassion, social justice, and environmental

stewardship. Creating communities that are inclusive, supportive, and equitable.
*   **Political and Economic Reform:** Implementing policies that address systemic inequalities, promote economic justice, and protect the environment. Strengthening international institutions and promoting global cooperation.

This vision of a compassionate future is not merely a desirable outcome; it is a necessity for the survival and flourishing of humanity. By redefining civilization based on compassion, empathy, and social justice, we can create a world where human progress is truly aligned with human well-being. This is the challenge and the opportunity of our time. It is a call to build a truly civilized world.